Primer Level
(Early Elementary)

Little Animal Tunes

By John W. Schaum

Arranged by Wesley Schaum and Jeff Schaum

I0792802

Foreword

This charming collection of songs is about eleven young animals and birds. The lyrics include interesting facts about their lives. Several birds are included because, according to definition, an animal is a generic term including any living thing that eats and moves around by itself.

Students may be aware that the titles can apply to other animals. For example, a *calf* can also be a cow, giraffe, whale, buffalo, camel, caribou, moose, etc. A *kitten* can be a lion, tiger, leopard, cougar ocelot and others. *Chicks* can be an ostrich, pelican, chicken, etc.

Each piece includes hand position diagrams at the top. The music has a minimum of finger numbers. The pieces span the primer level and are grouped in order of gradually increasing difficulty. Duet accompaniments are provided for teacher, parent, or older student to play along. However, the student should be comfortable with the solo part before adding the duet accompaniment.

Index

Schaum Publications, Inc.
10235 N. Port Washington Rd. • Mequon, WI 53092
www.schaumpiano.net

10-15

Duet Accompaniment

Note: In these accompaniments, notes with *stem up* are to be played with the *right* hand. Notes with *stem down* are to be played with the *left* hand.

PUPPIES

L. H. Position
R. H. Position
Moderato
Young pup - pies romp a lot. They love to play.
Young pup - pies need to learn. They must o - bey.
When they are grown up dogs, They make good pals.
Dogs can be help - ful too, They guard our home.

Duet Accompaniment

DUCKLINGS

L. H. Position
R. H. Position
Allegretto
mf
Four duck - lings wad - dling a - long the lake shore,
All seek - ing new things for them to ex - plore.
Fol - low - ing moth - er duck swim in the lake,
They all stay close be - hind for safe - ty's sake.

Duet Accompaniment

CALF

L. H. Position
R. H. Position
Maestoso
ff
There's a new born calf, It's an el - e - phant.
When it's ful - ly grown, It may weigh five tons.
f
El - e - phants are ver - y strong. They pull cir - cus wag - ons.
ff
They're in - tel - li - gent, They learn to per - form.

Duet Accompaniment

FOALS

L. H. Position
R. H. Position
Animato
A foal of course grows in - to a horse. All
foals have goals, they work hard all day. They
learn to trot and prance and gal - lop. Some
day real soon they'll be on pa - rade.

Duet Accompaniment

GOSLINGS

L. H. Position
R. H. Position
Moderato
mp
Lit - tle gos - lings crack their egg shells, That's how they break out, you see.
With their bright black eyes they peek out, Gaz - ing hap - pi - ly.
In the nest their par - ents feed them, Guard - ing them from an - y harm.
When it's cold they're well pro - tec - ted, Un - der - neath their par - ents' wings.

Duet Accompaniment

KITTENS

L. H. Position
R. H. Position
Andante
p
Here kit - ty, here kit - ty, come kit - ty, come.
Break - fast is read - y so come kit - ty, come.
Hur - ry now kit - ty, come run kit - ty, run.
Come get your break - fast, O come kit - ty, come!

Duet Accompaniment

CYGNETS

L. H. Position
R. H. Position
Allegretto
mp
Cyg - nets swim - ming in the pond,
Stay - ing close to moth - er swan,
In the qui - et of the dawn,
Guard - ing them is pa - pa swan.
Cyg - nets swim - ming round and round,
Sel - dom walk - ing on the ground.
Near their par - ents they'll be found,
Cyg - nets rare - ly make a sound.

Duet Accompaniment

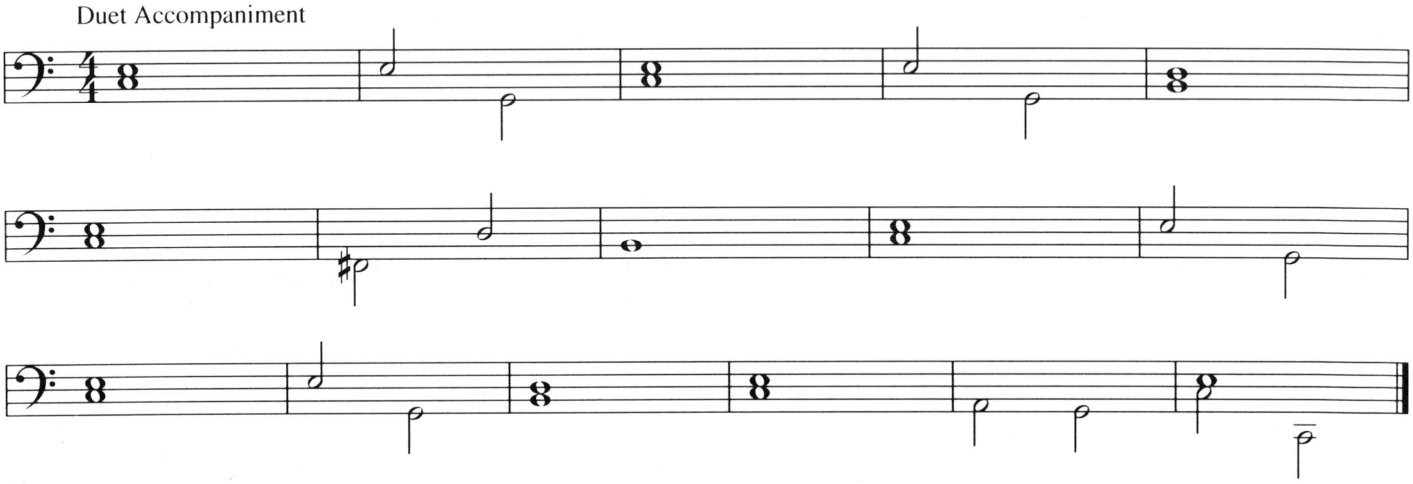

CHICKS

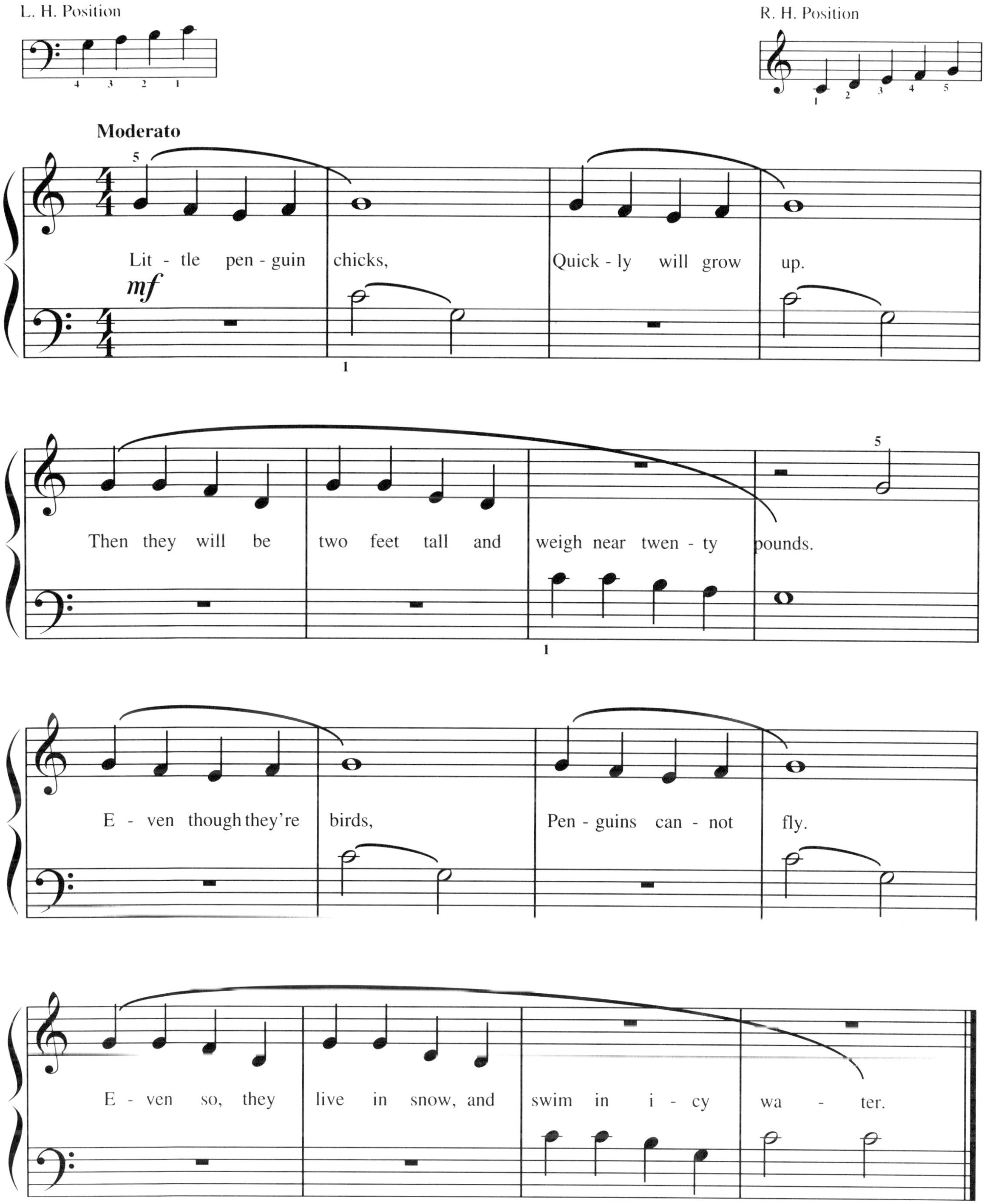
L. H. Position
R. H. Position
Moderato
mf
Lit - tle pen - guin chicks,
Quick - ly will grow up.
Then they will be two feet tall and weigh near twen - ty pounds.
E - ven though they're birds,
Pen - guins can - not fly.
E - ven so, they live in snow, and swim in i - cy wa - ter.

Duet Accompaniment

FAWNS

L. H. Position
R. H. Position
Andantino
mf
Lit - tle fawns are ver-y dear friends, 'Cause their par - ents are dears.
Some deer help at hol-i-day time, They are known as rein - deer.
They have hoofs es - pe-cial-ly made for pat - ter - ing on roof - tops.
In the win - ter when it is cold, Deer find food be - neath the snow.

Duet Accompaniment

LAMBS

L. H. Position
R. H. Position
Allegretto
Some-times lambs are frisk - y, Some-times they are wild.
Some-times lambs are gen - tle, Some-times they are mild.
Most times they are eat - ing, That's the way they grow.
Grown up lambs are sheep, you know, and they pro - vide our wool.

Duet Accompaniment

JOEYS

L. H. Position

R. H. Position